Leading with a
Humble Heart

Leading with a Humble Heart

A 40-Day Devotional for Leaders

Zac Bauermaster

ConnectEDD Publishing
Hanover, Pennsylvania

This publication is available at discount pricing when purchased in quantity for educational purposes, promotions, or fundraisers. For inquiries and details, contact the publisher at
info@connecteddpublishing.com

Published by ConnectEDD Publishing LLC
Hanover, PA
www.connecteddpublishing.com

Cover Design: Kheila Dunkerly

Leading with a Humble Heart/Zac Bauermaster. —1st ed.
Paperback ISBN 979-8-9860690-2-9

Praise for *Leading with a Humble Heart*...

"*Leading with a Humble Heart* is a call for leaders to humbly face the challenges of leadership through a confidence only found in God. Zac shares personal leadership experiences combined with Bible stories to exemplify there is nothing more impactful than a humble leader rooted in their faith in God."

—Jon Gordon | best-selling author of *The Carpenter* and *The Power of Positive Leadership*

"In *Leading with a Humble Heart*, Zac Bauermaster authentically challenges leaders to step outside the familiar to maximize the God-given gifts and abilities they've been given. Far too often, leaders cling to what is familiar and miss out on what they have been called to do. Throughout the 40-day journey, Zac shares personal stories of fear, doubt, and uncertainty combined with scripture verses and reflection questions to help leaders see that true confidence begins with humbling ourselves before the Lord, recognizing we can do nothing apart from Him. *Leading with a Humble Heart* points leaders back to solitary time with our Heavenly Father in Word and prayer for transformational leadership and ultimately advancing God's Kingdom."

—Bob Goff | Author of New York Times Bestsellers, *Love Does*, *Everybody Always*, *Dream Big* and *Undistracted*

"Zac Bauermaster has very insightfully and passionately handed us the keys to Kingdom leadership in this brilliant devotional. In our modern culture where the impatient need for fast paced results has even invaded the church, Zac invites us back into a place of rest and humility, remembering those who wait upon The Lord shall renew their strength. Follow Zac's lead back into the secret place where true Spirit led leaders are born!"

—Mark Graalman | Founding Member/Drummer of *Sanctus Real*

"Leaders who don't reflect, refresh, and replenish will eventually burn out. In *Leading with a Humble Heart*, Zac points us to the ultimate source of restoration. No doubt it will be water to the thirsty leader's soul. I hope that as you begin this journey, you find (as I did) a renewed sense of grace and peace."

> —Peter Greer | President & CEO, HOPE International and co-author *The Gift of* Disillusionment

"*Leading with a Humble Heart* is a guidebook for anyone looking for courage and inspiration on their leadership journey. With daily bible readings, journal prompts, and relatable, personal stories from Zac, this devotional is a wonderful tool to reflect on one's calling and remind aspiring, new, and veteran leaders of their purpose and core values."

> —Jennifer Hogan | 2018 Alabama Assistant Principal of the Year, Facilitator for The Hope Institute, Host of the *Communities of Character* podcast

"This devotional is the exact book that should be in the hands of leaders everywhere. *Leading with a Humble Heart* will encourage you to slow down, be still, and focus on one leadership challenge at a time through the lens of scripture. As leaders, we are trusted to follow our callings and use our gifts, and this devotional is an excellent guide whether you are just starting your leadership journey or needing some guidance along the way. Begin reading today if you are ready to tackle challenges with a gentle heart and humble confidence."

> —Kayla Dornfeld | 2019 North Dakota Teacher of the Year, 2020 USA Educator of the Year, CEO Top Dog Teaching Inc.

"Faithful leadership requires us to pause and process in a world with competing priorities. Many leaders struggle to make the space in their already full calendars to do what we know will serve our spirits. In

Leading with a Humble Heart, Zac Bauermaster has created a tool to ground leaders in a 40-day devotional which weaves scripture and real-life leadership connections that are relatable and relevant. What a gift from Zac's humble heart to ours with his reflection prompts, further reading, and 7-S Framework! This message offers a fresh perspective to help you make that intentional space to ignite your ability to lead with a strong spirit every day."

—Sarah Johnson | author *Lead with FAITH: Building a Strong Foundation So You Can Rise Up, Slay Fear*, and *Serve Well*

"Zac gives us a powerful reminder that a humble heart found through God's word and prayer gives us true confidence. There are scripture passages and additional readings to get leaders in the Word of God including authentic, real stories of many internal challenges leaders face but many do not share. In our packed schedule/ chaotic world ,the reflection questions help us to slow down and really think about our individual walks with the Lord and our leadership."

—Jeff Rutt | CEO Keystone Custom Homes, Chairman/Founder, HOPE International

"Everything that qualifies someone for leadership is directly related to character. In *Leading with a Humble Heart*, Zac provides a faith-based roadmap for leaders looking for true confidence that can only be found by humbling ourselves before God. This 40-Day devotional interweaves relevant scripture from the Bible, stories from Zac's personal journey, along with reflective and thought-provoking questions to deepen your walk with the Lord. *Leading with a Humble Heart* will better prepare you for your leadership roles in a way that makes a profound impact on those around you and honors God. A true must read."

—Jonathan Alsheimer | Teacher, Speaker, Author of *Next Level Teaching*

"It's easier said than done to face our giants with confidence. In Zac Bauermaster's *Leading with a Humble Heart: A 40-Day Devotional for Leaders*, Zac provides the reader with the armor to face our giants with a process to quiet ourselves and the noise of our world. The 40-day devotional breathes a structure that includes scripture, Zac's transparent and vulnerable life stories, a Biblical leadership connection, additional Bible readings, and questions for the reader's connection and reflection. The time is now for intentional spiritual growth so make today your Day 1. Prepare to face your giants and journey with Zac, as you lead with a humble heart.

—Stacey Green | Nationally Distinguished Principal

"Being an educational leader is extremely difficult and it requires various forms of support to be successful. *Leading with a Humble Heart: A 40-Day Devotional for Leaders* is an amazing tool to guide you with scripture, journal prompts, and additional resources. If you are looking to enhance your spiritual gifts, love, and compassion as a leader, this is the book for you!"

—Joshua Stamper | Administrator, author, speaker, podcaster, and the Training and Development Specialist for the Teach Better Team

"Leading with a Humble Heart is a devotional for leaders in all industries. Each day not only engages but also strengthens and sharpens a leader's faith journey. God's transformation will be evident in the lives of leaders who sit down each morning with God and use Zac's 7-S Framework in correlation to the devotion."

—Garret Barbush | Chief Communications Mentor, *Men of Iron* (www.menofiron.org)

"Zac Bauermaster has written a must-read devotional for any leader desiring to improve themselves and have a more profound impact on those they lead. *Leading With a Humble Heart* will empower you to reflect on your leadership journey, apply relevant scripture, and use thoughtful explorations to transform your leadership!"

—Wade Stanford | Westwood ISD Superintendent

"Servant leaders meet the thirst of those before them in countless ways, but where do such leaders go to replenish their own well—before the well goes dry? Rooted in scripture, enhanced through real-life examples, prompted by reflective journaling, *Leading with a Humble Heart* can help any leader "replenish the well" through the *living water* available through Jesus Christ and the Holy Spirit."

—Dr. Joe Schroeder | Associate Executive Director, Association of Wisconsin School Administrators (AWSA)

"*Leading with a Humble Heart* is a powerful and practical forty-day devotional for leaders! Zac's use of biblical accounts, the insight of others, and personal experiences make each day's leadership focus impactful and relatable. It's inspiring and encouraging for leaders whether experienced or just beginning the adventure."

—Blake Deibler | Lead Pastor, Wesley Church

"Have you ever as a disciple and servant leader of God felt him nudge you into a furious windstorm onto the Sea of Galilee. Did you feel alone in your leadership boat? Maybe one minute you felt the calmness of HIM praying in the mountains and the next the waves were more than you could handle. In Zac Bauermaster's Book, *Leading with a Humble Heart: A 40-Day Devotional for Leaders*, he not only meekly walks on water with leaders with his purposeful words of inspiration, but reminds them not to be afraid, to take courage, and to anchor down in the Godly moments of being still in their space to surrender, scribe, supplicate and most importantly serve faithfully."

—Megan Anderson | PreK-2 Assistant Principal at Cherry Hill Primary

"In the busyness and business of school leadership, *Leading with a Humble Heart* is the necessary pause leaders need in order to recalibrate, rest, and reset our focus and purpose in this work."

—Jessica Cabeen | Award Winning Principal, *SavED by Grace* Editor, Speaker, and Author

Dedication

In honor of my late grandfathers:

Robert M. Bauermaster
Elmer B. Wade

They left a family legacy of leading
with a humble heart rooted in Jesus.

To my wife and kids:

Carly, as I wrote this book, I realized more and more
why God put us together and placed you by my side. Thank you
for your daily wisdom, love, and encouragement. I love you.

Olivia, Eliot, and Isaac, God is your helper and in Him you
can do all things. Don't settle for what feels comfortable,
but allow the Lord to stretch you, and watch how
much you grow in Him. Be different. I love you.

Table of Contents

Preface

Pause and take a deep breath. Leadership is hard, isn't it? Leadership can undoubtedly be a roller coaster full of highs and lows. As I write this, it is 4:30 in the morning after a night of not sleeping well due to some difficult situations at work and some conversations ahead. On top of being a school leader, I am a husband, parent to three children, coach, and active member of my church. Everywhere I turn, there seem to be more and more responsibilities, often leaving me feeling stressed, anxious, and overwhelmed, wondering if I can even do it all. I am sure many of you have been there yourselves.

As John Maxwell says, "Leadership is influence, nothing more and nothing less" (Maxwell, 2015). You have this book in your hand because you have influence; you are a leader. This devotional book is for leaders from any walk of life looking to learn, grow, and improve themselves and those they lead. Throughout the book you may see leadership through my school leadership lens, but leadership is leadership, and this devotional book is for leaders in any role. Whether you are a business owner, lead a non-profit, a pastor, a teacher, mother, father, coach, male or female, this devotional book is for you.

When it comes to leadership, we often neglect the book that can truly transform our hearts, thus transforming ourselves, our relationships, and our leadership: the bare Word of God. I began writing this devotional book as I saw every leadership situation, challenge, success, hardship, and difficulty pointing me to the scriptures. While many leadership books inform, the Bible transforms. It is filled with leaders who both triumphed when walking with the Lord and experienced significant failure for trying to lead and do things independently from Him. However, one leader stood above the rest, Jesus. What began with personal leadership experiences, early morning journaling, and quiet time with the Lord in prayer and His Word, transformed into this leadership devotional book.

This devotional book aims to quiet ourselves as leaders, help us be still each morning, and allows us to spend 40 days with God in His word, reflecting on our leadership for transformational leadership wisdom. The number 40 is mentioned in the Bible numerous times and generally symbolizes a period of testing, trials, and triumphs. Leadership is complex, and leaders often experience significant trials and testing periods. You may be coming out of a recent leadership trial, in the midst of one, or heading into a challenging leadership season. Below are a few examples of 40-day or 40-year trials and testing periods from the Bible:

1. The Israelites wandered in the desert for 40 years.
2. Moses was atop Mount Sinai for 40 days.
3. King Saul, David, and Solomon ruled for 40 years.
4. God flooded the earth for 40 days as Noah and his family remained on the Ark.
5. Goliath taunted Israel for 40 days before David defeated him.
6. Moses, Elijah, and Jesus fasted in the desert for 40 days.
7. There were 40 days between Jesus' resurrection and ascension to Heaven.

Leading with a Humble Heart is an invitation for leaders to stare the challenges of leadership in the face through humility and confidence that can only be found in God's Word and prayer. By intentionally being in God's Word and prayer each day, God will not only equip us to face the challenges and tests of leadership; but we will also learn to thrive in those moments and seasons as we operate from a position of humble confidence. *Humble enough to know that, apart from Christ, we can do nothing, and confident enough to know we can do all things through Christ.*

How Each Day Works

*L*eading with a Humble Heart is driven by scripture and authentic leadership stories and experiences from the author, with practical points of reflection and application. The devotional book includes various leadership topics from a Biblical lens centered around humility and confidence. Each day consists of a title, scripture verse, additional reading, a personal leadership story, and a biblical leadership example. The scripture passages for the devotional are taken from the New International Version (NIV) translation of the bible. Lastly, *Leading with a Humble Heart* has a built-in journaling area allowing readers to reflect and journal.

However, this leadership devotional book is not simply about sitting down, reading a devotion, jotting down a few words in a journal, and moving on with your day. This devotional is about transforming your heart as a leader through daily, intentional time with the Heavenly Father. I recognize many people struggle with where to start when it comes to prayer and scripture reading, often preventing them from developing a habit of carving out time with God. Therefore, I also wanted to share a **7 S- Framework** for quiet time I developed and use each morning myself. Like the number 40, seven is also a Biblically significant number as it represents fullness or completion. Feel free to give the framework a try over the next 40 days and see if it works for you. Lastly, if you miss a day, keep going. As the legendary Tony Dungy said, *"Yesterday is gone, spend time with God today"* (Dungy, 2011).

7-S Framework for Quiet Time with God

Space: Be intentional about creating space to spend time with God and in His Word. If you can, try and wake up a little earlier and spend time in the quietness of the morning. I recognize that will not work for everyone's schedule, so find what works for you. Like me, I hope you will come to see this as the favorite part of your day.

> Mark 1:35- Very early in the morning, while it was still dark, Jesus got up, left the house, and went off to a solitary place, where he prayed.

Stillness: Now that you have created space, quiet your heart before the Lord. This is where your mind may be running with everything you have to do each day or reflecting on what happened the day before. For some, you will be fighting that feeling that you have too much to do to sit down. Take a deep breath as you start each day in the humble confidence of Exodus 14:14.

> Exodus 14:14 - The Lord will fight for you; you need only to be still.

Surrender: Humility is essential to leadership. As you sit in the stillness, surrender to the Lord in prayer, preparing your heart to absorb God's Word, recognizing He is in control of everything. Surrender each day by acknowledging we can do nothing apart from God.

> John 15:5 - "I am the vine; you are the branches. If you remain in me and I in you, you will bear much fruit; apart from me you can do nothing."

Study: Now that you have created space, are still, and have surrendered, dive into the scripture verse(s) and devotional for the day and spend time in the Word of God.

> Hebrews 4:12 - For the word of God is alive and active. Sharper than any double-edged sword, it penetrates even to dividing soul and spirit, joints and marrow; it judges the thoughts and attitudes of the heart.

Scribe: After studying the Word and spending time reading, it is time to write. Journal daily.

Psalm 102:18 - Let this be written for a future generation, that a people not yet created may praise the Lord.

Supplication: Close in prayer, humbly asking God for his divine help, that he would give you the confidence, strength, wisdom, and discernment you need for each day.

Philippians 4:6 - Do not be anxious about anything, but in everything by prayer and supplication with thanksgiving, let your requests be known to God.

Serve: Lastly, head out into wherever God has called you to use your leadership gifts, serving Him and others humbly and confidently. God is your strength!

1 Peter 4:10 - Each of you should use whatever gift you have received to serve others, as faithful stewards of God's grace in its various forms.

I pray that not only will the next 40 days transform your leadership, but most importantly, transform your heart. As we will see over the next 40 days, our words, thoughts, and actions reflect our hearts and can significantly impact those we lead. I pray that we all lead with a heart of humble confidence. Thank you for joining me on this journey.

Day 1

_____•_____

Way Too Busy Not to Pray

Today's Verse: Mark 1:35 - Very early in the morning, while it was still dark, Jesus got up, left the house, and went off to a solitary place, where he prayed.

My mind is constantly moving in all different directions. When I wake up early in the morning, or sit down to spend time with God, my mind is often pulled to everything else I "need" to do or could be doing during that time. Unfortunately, that anxious feeling often leads me to limit my time with God as I struggle with a constant feeling of needing to get other things done. Marshall Segal said it this way, "Satan will try to make everything feel more urgent than sitting down to be with Jesus" (Segal, 2021). Instead of allowing myself to be quiet and still before the Lord, I try to push even harder to complete everything I need to do, leaving me feeling unsettled, anxious, discontent, and drained.

During His time on earth, Jesus set a perfect example of restoring Himself to continue His mission. Jesus was often with large crowds, preaching the good news and healing. People came from all over to be with Jesus. They wanted to be close to Him, hear from Him, and be healed by Him. In response, Jesus knew exactly what He needed to do.

As Mark 1:35 states, Jesus would often get up early in the morning and find a solitary place to pray to his Heavenly Father. Jesus knew how important quiet time with the Creator was-–the one who knew exactly what he needed each moment of every day. In his book, *C.H. Spurgeon on Spiritual Leadership*, Steve Miller shared a quote from Charles Spurgeon: "Sometimes we think we are too busy to pray. That is a great mistake, for praying is a way of saving time" (Miller, 2003). Jesus knew he could not do it on his own, and certainly neither can we. Our lives are way too busy not to pray.

Journal: How does following Jesus' example of spending solitary time in prayer with God change your perspective of prioritizing time in your day for solitude and prayer? Where can you find time in your day for solitude or prayer? How does this impact the other things you "need" to do?

Additional Reading: Mark 1

Day 2

Rest in Him

Today's Verse: Genesis 2:2 - By the seventh day God had finished the work he had been doing, so on the seventh day he rested from all his work.

I tend to be more anxious when I am not working than when I am actually working. In Alan Fadling's book, *An Unhurried Leader* (Fadling, 2017), he uses the example of an old childhood toy, the Chinese finger trap, to illustrate how leaders respond to stress and anxiousness. When a child places their fingers in the trap, the trap tightens. The child's initial response is to pull even harder to escape, ultimately tightening the trap even more. The Chinese finger trap exemplifies how leaders often try to outwork their stress. As we saw in yesterday's reading, when I feel overwhelmed or stressed, I try to push through and do even more, which only compacts the stress. The vicious cycle leaves me tired, anxious, and often with a poor attitude. I have realized how this unhealthy rhythm is prideful and exposes my lack of trust in my Heavenly Father as I fear I will fall behind if I do not keep pushing ahead every day.

During the seventh day of creation, God rested. God created a pattern of work and rest through the seven days of creation. God certainly did not need rest on the seventh day because he was tired. His rest showed His work was finished and gave a pattern to man regarding the structure of time. God's seven-day design exemplifies the blessing of rest to man on the seventh day. As David says in Psalm 23:2, "He makes me lie down in green pastures, he leads me beside quiet waters." Much like sheep, we do not always know what we need, but God as the Good Shepherd knows exactly what we need, including resting in Him. As leaders, we ought to rest as hard as we work, resting in Him.

Journal: Oftentimes as leaders we work tirelessly towards tasks or accomplishments and never make time to rest and enjoy the fruits of our work. How can God's seven-day pattern of creation create a healthy rhythm of work and rest to strengthen your leadership?

Additional Reading: Genesis 1, Genesis 2:1-3, Psalm 23

Day 3

———— • ————

Present and Future

Today's Verse: Genesis 41:35 - They should collect all the food of these good years that are coming and store up the grain under the authority of Pharaoh, to be kept in the cities for food.

Vision is one of the most commonly used terms when discussing leadership. Solomon says in Proverbs 29:18, "Where there is no vision, the people perish." As leaders, we are not only to be in the moment, but we must also look ahead to see how we can best provide for the people in and around our homes, schools, teams, or organizations. I recently talked to a leader who was asked to present a five-year vision for a district as part of the interview process for a school superintendent position. The committee was not simply interested in what he would bring to the school district immediately, but more importantly, his vision and strategy for moving the school district forward.

In the story of Joseph, if there had been no vision, the people certainly would have perished. Joseph interpreted Pharaoh's dreams, allowing for seven years of abundance followed by seven years of famine. It is important to note when Pharaoh asked Joseph to interpret his dreams, Joseph humbly responded, "I cannot do it, but God will give Pharoah the answer he desires" (v. 16). Genesis 41:31 says the abundance in the land will not be remembered, because the famine that follows it will be so severe. During the seven years of plenty, Joseph and the people collected all the food produced in Egypt and stored it in the cities. Joseph stored up such large quantities of grain that they quit keeping records because it was beyond measure (v. 49). However, just as quickly as the seven years of abundance started, the seven years of famine began. Due to Joseph's faith and action, although there was famine in all other lands, there was food in the whole land of Egypt (v. 53). Leading through the present while looking towards the future is a significant challenge, but an even greater opportunity.

Journal: How can Joseph's example of vision, strategy, and execution guide you in your leadership when difficult times arise? Is there a challenge you are currently facing where Joseph's example can be instrumental in providing you the forethought to lead people through it?

Additional Reading: Genesis 41

Day 4

———— • ————

God's Never Early;
He's Never Late

Today's Verse: Genesis 41:41 - So Pharaoh said to Joseph, "I hereby put you in charge of the whole land of Egypt."

God's timing is perfect. As a human, I naturally want things to occur when I think they should. Simply put, waiting can be hard. There were various times I interviewed for jobs when I thought the timing was perfect; I thought the positions were meant to be. However, God had a different plan. Additionally, we often experience challenges or difficulties during those times of waiting. God uses those times of waiting to continue preparing and shaping our hearts for the mission and tasks he has set out for us. It is humbling to reflect back to those moments where we thought something was meant to be, and God keeps that door closed. As Toby Mac's song, *Help is on the Way*, exclaims, "God's never early, never late" (McKeehan, 2021). The story of Joseph in Genesis is a perfect example of God's timing, not our own.

Let's look at everything that led up to Joseph being put in charge of the whole land of Egypt. First, Joseph's brothers were jealous and sold him into slavery, telling their father that Joseph had been killed. The Midianites then sold Joseph to Potiphar, one of Pharaoh's officials. Next, Joseph was wrongly accused of making advancements towards Potiphar's wife and was thrown in jail. Joseph was then forgotten in prison by the cupbearer. Eventually, the chief cupbearer remembered Joseph in prison, and Pharaoh brought Joseph up to interpret his dreams. Joseph interpreted the dreams which allowed Egypt to embrace seven years of abundance in preparation for seven years of severe famine. Altogether, it had been thirteen years since Joseph was sold into slavery until he was put in charge of Egpyt. I am sure that was not the path Joseph had in mind when he first dreamt of the sun, moon, and stars bowing down to him or when his father Israel gave him the coat of many colors (Genesis 37:3). However, he remained faithful to God during the wait, and the Lord was with him. Wait patiently and trust God, He's never early, He's never late.

Journal: Impatience frequently leads us away from our faith in Christ. Think of the ways in which your impatience leads to a lack of effectiveness in your work and draws you away from the leader you desire to be. How can you turn your times of waiting into opportunities for prayer in order to be more strategic and exemplify your humble confidence?

Additional Reading: Genesis 41

Day 5

Speak Boldly in God's Confidence

Today's Verse: Exodus 4:11-12 - The Lord said to him, "Who gave man his mouth? Who makes him deaf or mute? Who gives him sight or makes him blind? Is it not I, the Lord? Now go; I will help you speak and will teach you what to say."

One day I shared with a friend how nervous I felt to speak to a large group. His response was simply, "Go spend some time reading Exodus Chapter 4". As leaders, we frequently speak publicly to groups, lead challenging meetings and conversations, or interview for a promotion. Although we may look confident on the outside, we often experience doubts and fears. Will we forget what to say? What if we do not say the right thing? How will people respond? Maybe there is someone better equipped to do this? Maybe we have past experiences that have caused us to lose confidence in ourselves. When those doubts and worries creep in, we begin focusing on our human abilities and limit the capabilities of Almighty God.

In Exodus 4, Moses faced similar fears, doubting his ability to speak. When called by God to approach Pharoah and lead the Israelites out of Egypt, Moses responded, "O Lord, I have never been eloquent, neither in the past nor since you have spoken to your servant. I am slow of speech and tongue (v. 4:10)." Moses' initial reaction was self-focused, leading to doubt of his abilities. Almighty God's response, "Who gave man his mouth?" Wow. That same Almighty God that gave Moses his mouth did the same for you. Get rid of self-confidence and speak boldly in God's confidence.

Journal: How does trusting in God's strength, the one "who gave man his mouth," and not on your own strength increase your humble confidence? How can Exodus 4 lead you from your doubts and into your calling while knowing your work is serving God here on Earth?

Additional Reading: Exodus 4

Day 6

---•---

We Can't Do It Alone

Today's Verse: Numbers 11:14 - I cannot carry all these people by myself; the burden is too heavy for me.

It can be easy to feel as though asking others for help is a sign of weakness, but this could not be further from the truth. A term that many leaders struggle to put into practice effectively is delegation. The definition of the term delegate is to "Entrust a task or responsibility to another person" (n.d.). Andy Stanley, Pastor and host of the Andy Stanley Leadership podcast describes leadership as, "Getting things done through other people" (Stanley, 2006). God has given us a unique set of talents and abilities, and when leaders empower others through delegation, we can multiply our success significantly. When we try to get things done ourselves, we not only exhaust ourselves, but we substantially limit the potential of those we lead. Delegation is about recognizing the gifts of others and empowering them with the tools to thrive.

God helped Moses recognize that leading Israel was far too big for him to do on his own. This was undoubtedly a good thing for Moses as he realized his limits and God's strength. Numbers 12:3 says that,

"Now Moses was a very humble man, more humble than anyone else on the face of the earth." He humbly cried out to the Lord, asking for help, "I cannot carry all these people by myself; the burden is too heavy for me (v. 14). The Lord heard Moses' request and said to him, "Bring me seventy of Israel's elders who are known to you as leaders and officials among the people (v. 16). They will help you carry the burden of the people so that you will not have to carry it alone (v. 17). Moses learned the importance of relying on God and empowering others through delegation. We can't do it alone.

Journal: How can the story of Moses encourage you to delegate and empower those around you as you realize your limitations and God's strength? Do those you empower know their capabilities and limitations? What positive outcomes might result through this delegation?

Additional Reading: Numbers 11, Numbers 12:3

Day 7

·—•—·

The Generations to Come

Today's Verse: Numbers 27:15-16 - Moses said to the Lord, "May the Lord, the God of the spirits of all mankind, appoint a man over the community."

Growing up, my family drove from Pennsylvania to Florida every Christmas. It was a 16-hour trip that often required driving through the night. As my mom and sisters would drift to sleep, I would stay awake talking and listening to my dad as he drove. I knew that one day, God-willing, I would have a family of my own, and it would be me in that driver's seat. He not only wanted to prepare me to stay awake traveling through the night to take care of my family, but most importantly, my dad spent my childhood equipping me to trust God, lead my family, and continue our family's legacy through "little" moments like those trips to Florida.

Moses knew his leadership was a temporary assignment, so he intentionally invested in other leaders, specifically Joshua. Moses served the Israelites by pouring himself into Joshua to ensure that the Israelites would continue to fear and love God. Joshua spent more than 40 years listening, observing, and leading under Moses before he took over Moses' role as the leader of Israel. After Moses led the Israelites out of Egypt through the wilderness, Joshua was more than prepared to lead them into the promised land after the death of Moses. Leadership is looking beyond ourselves and investing in the generations to come.

Journal: Like Moses, how are you investing and prioritizing time with those around you to ensure your legacy carries on even when you are gone? Who is a person in your leadership circle you need to spend more time with in order to move your mission forward?

Additional Reading: Numbers 27, Psalm 78: 1-8

Day 8

———— • ————

Develop Leaders,
Not Followers

Today's Verse: Judges 2: 8 and 10 - Joshua, son of Nun, the servant of the Lord, died at the age of a hundred and ten. After that whole generation had been gathered to their fathers, another generation grew up, who knew neither the Lord nor what he had done for Israel.

When I was a high school assistant principal I worked with a school superintendent who would say, "If I leave this district and things fall apart, then I have failed as a leader." He often stressed the importance of investing in district administrators, principals, and teacher leaders to continue to move the mission, vision, and core values forward. He ensured that leaders were developed, and effective systems were put into place for the school district to make progress and grow regardless of whether he was there. He was not looking to create a culture in which people followed the leader, but a culture in which people were developed into leaders.

Yesterday, we saw how much time Moses poured into Joshua preparing him to lead the Israelites. Unfortunately, the same cannot be said for Joshua. When Moses died, the Israelites continued full steam ahead and entered the promised land under the leadership of Joshua. However, Joshua did not invest time into developing leaders around him. After Joshua's death, the Israelites drifted from the Lord and lived in a time of chaos as a generation that did not know the Lord. Leaders develop leaders, not followers.

Journal: Joshua's story is a cautionary tale for leadership. Are you investing in developing leaders like Moses or Joshua? What investment do you need to commit to in your leadership to lead more like Moses and less like Joshua.

Additional Reading: Judges 2

Day 9

—————— • ——————

Lead from Overflow

Today's Verse: Judges 4:14- Then Deborah said to Barak, Go! This is the day the Lord has given Sisera into your hands. Has not the Lord gone ahead of you? So Barak went down Mount Tabor, with ten thousand men following him.

A Bible verse that has significantly impacted my life is Matthew 6:21, "For where your treasure is, there your heart will be also." This verse is a humbling reminder that God must be our treasure. Too often we search out other treasures to "fill our cups," such as money, success, or human praise and fail to keep in alignment with the one true treasure: Almighty God. In his book, *An Unhurried Leader*, Alan Fadling discusses leading from "overflow" (Fadling, 2017). When we make God our treasure, our leadership can flourish as we "fill our cups" from the vertical love of God and pass the overflow horizontally to those we lead.

Deborah, a Judge in Israel, made God her treasure. Deborah has been described as a "worshiping warrior." She was chosen to lead and serve God's people at a highly challenging time for the Israelites as they faced oppression from the Canaanites. Upon receiving instructions

17

from the Lord, Deborah called Barak to stand by her side and obeyed the Lord's commands as she inspired the Israelites to a victory over the Canaanite oppressors. However, this was not one moment in the making; this was Deborah day in and day out, making God her treasure. We ought to do the same, for where our treasure is, there our hearts will be. Go and lead from a position of "overflow."

Journal: Reflect on the story of Deborah and Matthew 6:21 - who or what is the treasure you are seeking? How can you lead from a position of "overflow" from God in your leadership?

Additional Reading: Judges 4, Matthew 6:21, Matthew 6:33

Day 10

Discomfort Leads to Growth

Today's Verse: Judges 7:2 - The Lord said to Gideon, "You have too many men for me to deliver Midian into their hands. In order that Israel may not boast against me that her own strength has saved her."

Paul says in 2 Corinthians 12:10, "That is why for Christ's sake, I delight in weaknesses, in insults, in hardships, in persecutions, in difficulties. For when I am weak, I am made strong." Weakness and vulnerability are not standard terms often embraced and associated with leadership. Before I faced a significant season of anxiety and depression, I was comfortable, simply going through the motions of life. God often puts us in situations where we realize growth and comfort cannot coexist. God had given me gifts and abilities, but I was not maximizing them to the fullest extent as I relied on my own strength. However, as uncomfortable as the anxiety and depression were, I knew God was in and above my circumstances. I came to realize how much He was shaping my heart and strengthening me for my leadership journey ahead.

It can be more difficult to rely on God when everything is going well, and we are blessed with abundant resources. God told Gideon, "The people with you are too many for me." Gideon must have been feeling uncomfortable because he had an army of 32,000 compared to 135,000 Midianites. God then commanded Gideon to invite all the troops who were afraid to go home. This left Gideon with 10,000 troops remaining. God told Gideon that there were still too many men, so Gideon led them to the water, where God tested them once again. Gideon's army was now reduced from 10,000 to 300. As they headed into battle significantly outnumbered by the Midianites, Gideon and his army could only trust in God, not themselves. In his book, *What Did You Expect*, Paul Tripp says, "Weakness is the portal to strength" (Tripp, 2010). God uses our human weakness to illuminate His strength. Next time you are feeling weak, delight in it and lean into God, discomfort leads to growth.

Journal: In leadership, weakness and discomfort can often be looked at negatively, but these can be valuable feelings in reminding us to rely on God. How can your current weaknesses and discomforts lead to a reliance on God? How will this reliance increase your faith and your effectiveness in your leadership?

Additional Reading: Judges 7, 2 Corinthians 12:10

Day 11

If I Fail, You Fail

Today's Verse: 1 Kings 3 : 7-9 - Now, O Lord my God, you have made your servant king in place of my father David. But I am only a little child and do not know how to carry out my duties. Your servant is here among the people you have chosen, a great people, too numerous to count or number. So give your servant a discerning heart to govern your people and to distinguish between right and wrong. For who is able to govern this people of yours.

It can be easy to battle doubt and uncertainty in our leadership roles, particularly when taking on the responsibilities of a new position or an unfamiliar task. We may look confident on the outside, but inside, leaders battle fear and take on the weight of leading others. A leader shared with me what he prays when called to a new task or position. "God, you have called me. If I fail, you fail." What is so powerful about that prayer is we already know the answer. God never fails, and His plan is perfect. It is a prayer of both humility and confidence.

The Lord asked King Solomon to ask for whatever he wanted, and God would provide (v.5). In response, Solomon humbled himself before the Lord, acknowledging God's goodness and faithfulness to him and his family. King Solomon knew the tasks ahead of him and humbly recognized that he could not carry them out apart from God. Solomon asked God for a discerning heart of wisdom to lead the Israelites with a heart that would listen to God and confidently trust in His plan. True confidence requires humility, and we must humble ourselves before the Lord acknowledging we can do nothing apart from Him. If we fail, He fails, and God never fails.

Journal: In our world today, the value of humility has been lessened a great deal. King Solomon was wise enough to recognize the role humility has in leadership and faith. How can you fight the urge to believe solely in yourself and humble yourself like King Solomon before the Lord acknowledging you can do nothing apart from Him? How can surrendering to God lead to confidence in your leadership?

Additional Reading: 1 Kings 3

Day 12

First Pray

Today's Verse: 1 Kings 22:5 - But Jehosaphat also said to the king of Israel, "First seek the counsel of the Lord."

Our days are often filled with decisions. A term called "decision fatigue" refers to the deteriorating quality of decisions after making many decisions throughout a day or week. How often do we make decisions without going to our Heavenly Father in prayer? Unfortunately for me, I know it is way too often. We have a direct line of communication to the Creator of the heavens and earth, the one who has all of our days written in His book (Psalm 139:16) and knows how many hairs are on our head (Luke 12:7). Our Father in Heaven knows exactly what we need each moment of each day, but all too often, we try to figure things out for ourselves.

During this time in Israel, there had been no war between Syria and Israel for three years. In the third year, Jehosaphat, King of Judah, visited the King of Israel, Ahab. There the King of Israel asked Jehosaphat to go with him to fight against Ramoth Gilead. Jehosaphat replied to the king of Israel, "First seek the counsel of the Lord," and proposed they seek God first regarding the matter. Jehosaphat knew that going to the one who made the heavens and the earth was a great place to start. He set an example we all can follow by his personal devotion to the Lord. No matter how big or how small our decisions may seem, first pray.

Journal: As leaders, decision making is an essential part of our daily lives. As you approach today and the many decisions you will be a part of or making directly, how will you take time to include the Lord in your decision-making process?

Additional Reading: 1 Kings 22, Luke 12, Psalm 139

Day 13

———— • ————

Don't Leave Any Arrows in Your Quiver

Today's Verse: 2 Kings 13: 18-19 - Then he said, "Take the arrows," and the king took them. Elisha told him, "Strike the ground." He struck it three times and stopped. The man of God was angry with him and said, "You should have struck the ground five or six times; then you would have defeated Aram and completely destroyed it. But now you will defeat it only three times."

One summer, I was interviewing for a new leadership position. I had served in various assistant leadership roles, but now I was interviewing to be a building principal. Imposter syndrome began to invade my head, "What if I can't do this?" One day I was sharing these concerns with my wife, and she looked at me and said, "Don't leave any arrows in your quiver." She knew God had equipped me with everything I needed to carry out His work, and if I did not continue to move forward for a new position, I would be wasting my God-given gifts and abilities.

In the passage in 2 Kings 13, we read that King Jehoash left arrows in his quiver, allowing only three victories over the Syrian army instead of the many more the Israelites could have enjoyed. King Jehoash received the prophet Elisha's invitation to "strike the ground" with timidness instead of bold confidence in the Lord. There are many situations in which we should "keep shooting our arrows," but timidness, doubt, and fear creep in, preventing us from maximizing what God has in store for our lives and the lives of those around us to advance His kingdom. For God did not give us a spirit of timidity, but of love, power, and self-discipline (2 Timothy 1:7). No regrets; don't leave any arrows in your quiver.

Journal: We often leave arrows in our quiver due to timidness, fear, doubt, and uncertainty. Are there any arrows you are hiding and what can you do to ensure you do not waste any of them?

Additional Reading: 2 Kings 13, 2 Timothy 1

Day 14

———•———

Day by Day,
Feed the Sheep

Today's Verse: 1 Samuel 16:11 - So he asked Jesse, "Are these all the sons you have?" There is still the youngest," Jesse answered, "but he is tending the sheep."

How do we trust God in the "big" things? We trust Him in the "little" things. We do not just graduate school, get a new job, become a CEO, superintendent, business owner, coach, spouse, or parent overnight. Instead, God shapes us through the mundane "little" moments of our daily lives, preparing us for those "big" moments. Our days, weeks, months, and years are certainly filled with mundane moments. Paul Tripp says, "You see, the character of a life is not set in two or three dramatic moments, but in 10,000 little moments. The character that was formed in those little moments is what shapes how you respond to the big moments of life" (Tripp, 2013).

When the Lord sent Samuel to Bethlehem to anoint one of Jesse's sons as the next King of Israel, David was nowhere to be found. He was a humble shepherd boy tending to his sheep in the fields. God had been shaping David's heart through the "little" moments of shepherding his flock of sheep in preparation for anointing him the next King of Israel. Day by day, David fed the sheep, trusting in God through the mundane moments of his life preparing his heart to respond to the "big" moments that lay ahead as King of Israel. We must remember that whether "big" or "little", every moment of our lives is shaping our hearts for what is to come. No moment is too big or too small; feed the sheep in what God has called you to do today.

Journal: Like David shepherding the sheep, leadership has many mundane tasks we participate in each day. How can we invite or recognize God into these tasks and these "little moments" to help build us into stronger leaders?

Additional Reading: 1 Samuel 16

Day 15

---•---

Face Your Giants
with Confidence

Today's Verse: 1 Samuel 17:32 - David said to Saul, "Let no one lose heart on account of the Philistine; your servant will go fight him."

Max Lucado once said, "Don't measure the height of the mountain; ponder the power of the one who made it" (Lucado, 2021.) We often look at situations through our human lens when facing an obstacle or challenge in leadership. Instead of looking at the One who made and can move the mountain, we look at the giant mountain in front of us. Trusting in our human perspective significantly reduces our view of the Almighty God and the leadership actions that follow. We limit ourselves and our God-given gifts and abilities in leadership far too often by choosing to lean on our own understanding, not His.

It can be easy to view the story of David and Goliath as a true underdog story. When all the other Israelites saw Goliath, they ran away from him in fear (v. 24). However, David saw things differently; he offered to fight Goliath because he knew it would be Almighty God versus puny Goliath, not the other way around. David stood with confidence because the Lord had prepared him for this battle while he was a lowly shepherd fighting lions and battling bears. David said to Goliath, "You come against me with sword and spear and javelin, but I come against you in the name of the Lord Almighty" (v. 45). Let's use David's example and face our "giants" with confidence!

Journal: David's perspective is impressive because while facing an earthly problem he took into account the divine. As leaders, facing challenges is part of our daily routine. Most of these challenges we face strictly with an earthly perspective. How can we begin to take David's perspective when facing our "giants." What is one challenge you may face today or in the future during which you will need to embrace the David-like perspective?

Additional Reading: 1 Samuel 17

Day 16

Don't Get Distracted

Today's Verse: 1 Kings 11:4 - As Solomon grew old, his wives turned his heart after other gods, and his heart was not fully devoted to the Lord his God.

Too often we have read, seen, or experienced a prominent leader spend their lifetime building a Godly, well-respected reputation, only to become distracted and lose that reputation in what looks like an "instant." Craig Groeschel, pastor of Life Church and host of the Craig Groeschel Leadership Podcast said, "The devil doesn't need to destroy you if he can distract you" (Groeschel, 2018). Some have experienced it first-hand; others have seen those stories on the internet or the news. Sadly, I have seen a few leaders lose their jobs, marriages, children, and even go to jail for their poor decisions. Our distractions can also seem minor on the outside. Maybe it's social media, a television series, or gossip that can quickly cause us to become distracted. When we lose sight of God's commands, it can happen to any of us.

Today's verse is a perfect example of how easily we can become distracted. This verse cannot be about the same King Solomon that God made "wiser than any other man," can it? The same King Solomon who "from all nations people came to listen to his wisdom" (1 Kings 4:34)? Unfortunately, it is. King Solomon did not heed God's warning and became distracted by women. His heart was not entirely devoted to the Lord as the heart of his father, David, and he turned to other gods. Ultimately, once wiser than any other man, Solomon did evil in the eyes of the Lord and did not follow him completely (v. 6). What may seem small at first can expand quickly; don't get distracted.

Journal: Distractibility negatively influences our effectiveness as leaders and more importantly, our faith. Who in your life helps you stay focused? Is there someone in your life you can help stay focused and avoid distractions?

Additional Reading: 1 Kings 11, Ephesians 6:10-18, Proverbs 27:17

Day 17

Impressive Empathy

Today's Verse: 1 Kings 12:8 - But Rehoboam rejected the advice the elders gave to him and consulted the young men who had grown up with him and were serving him.

In his book, *Change Leader*, Michael Fullan describes impressive empathy as the ability to understand those who disagree with you (Fullan, 2011). That is not an easy task and is a unique skill to master. Unfortunately, when faced with making decisions, we have the tendency to seek out information to support our pre-existing views and ideas, a term known as confirmation bias. We negatively impact our leadership potential when we only seek out views that align with ours and surround ourselves with people who think like us. Solomon says in Proverbs 12:15, "The way of the fool seems right to him, but the wise man listens to advice."

After Rehoboam became King of Israel, the people of Israel approached him and asked that he lighten the harsh labor and heavy yoke his father, King Solomon, had put on them (v. 4). Rehoboam initially responded appropriately; he asked for time to gather more information and consulted with the elders (v. 5-7). The elders told

Rehoboam to serve the people, give them a favorable answer, "and they will always be your servants" (v. 9). However, the elders' response was not what Rehoboam wanted to hear, and he went to seek advice from friends he had grown up with. Rehoboam's friends told him what he wanted to hear, "Make the yoke even heavier for the people" (v. 11). Rehoboam rejected the counsel of his elders and followed the advice of his friends leading Israel to rebellion against the House of David. We need to put away confirmation bias and lead with impressive empathy.

Journal: What is a big decision you are currently weighing for your family or organization? Who can you seek out that will offer an alternate view of the direction you are anticipating? Challenge yourself to listen to their perspective and utilize your impressive empathy lens to help make an even better decision.

Additional Reading: 1 Kings 12

Day 18

---•---

Every Unsung
Hero Matters

Today's Verse: 1 Samuel 30:21 - Then David came to the two hundred men who had been too exhausted to follow him and were left behind at Bestor Ravine. They came out to meet David and the people with him. As David and his men approached, he greeted them.

Many of the most impactful leaders know how to make every person in an organization feel special. These leaders can be found in the back of the kitchen spending time with the cafeteria staff, laughing and connecting with the custodial staff, forming meaningful relationships with everyone, no matter their role. One leader I spoke with described it this way, "Our organization is one big puzzle, and every person within the organization is a piece to that puzzle. If there is a piece missing, the puzzle is not complete. We need everyone."

King David recognized the importance of those who do thankless jobs. He knew for Israel to flourish; every role was essential. David took the time to connect with the "unsung heroes," the ones that many leaders would not think twice about. As today's verse describes, David took the time to greet two hundred men who had been left behind. King David experienced great success because through his faithfulness to God, he valued and appreciated every person. King David knew that everyone mattered and so should we. Don't let any of your "puzzle pieces" go to waste. Every "unsung hero" matters.

Journal: All pieces matter. As a leader, how can you connect, recognize, and celebrate the unsung heroes within your home, team, or organization to let them know they are valuable pieces to the puzzle?

Additional Reading: 1 Samuel 30

Day 19

Don't Go Idle

Today's Verse: 2 Samuel 11:1 - In the spring, at the time when kings go off to war, David sent Joab out with the king's men and the whole Israelite army. They destroyed the Ammonites and besieged Rabbah. But David remained in Jerusalem.

Idleness can be a dangerous thing. Typically, I pride myself on being self-controlled and disciplined. However, I become easily distracted when I have idle time and am more susceptible to temptation and sin. I saw a quote from Carey Neiuwhof that resonated with me: "When you're tired, bad things seem good and good things seem bad, and that's a perfect set-up for moral failure" (Neiuwhof, 2022). We often find Satan lurking around us during those times of tiredness and idleness. 1 Peter 5:8 says, "Be alert and of sober mind. Your enemy, the devil, prowls around like a roaring lion looking for someone to devour."

King David was indeed a "Man after God's own heart." However, 2 Samuel 11 and the sins of David exemplify that we are all sinners, and no one is immune to temptation and sin when unguarded. It was the spring, and King David should have been off to war with the rest of the kings, and instead, he chose to disobey God and remain in Israel. By staying in Israel, David gave into his idleness and the sins of the flesh. King David saw a woman bathing on the roof; he sent for her, slept with her, then worked diligently to cover his sin with more sins. We must put on the armor of God daily to resist the schemes of the evil one. As we see with King David, no one is immune to sin. Don't go idle.

Journal: Idleness often takes us away from our faith and our ideal leadership behavior. How have you seen or felt idleness impact your walk with the Lord and your leadership? What are ways you can turn your idleness into moments of devotion or necessary recharging?

Additional Reading: 1 Samuel 11, 1 Thessalonians 5, 1 Peter 5:8

Day 20

---•---

The Blame Game: Own It

Today's Verse: 1 Samuel 13:11-12 - "What have you done?" asked Samuel. Saul replied, "When I saw that the men were scattering, and that you did not come at the set time, and that the Philistines were assembling at Micmash, I thought, "Now the Philistines will come down against me at Gilgal, and I have not sought the Lord's favor. So I felt compelled to offer the burnt offering."

Ownership is a crucial characteristic of leadership. A school superintendent I worked with spoke about creating a culture of "extreme ownership." From the beginning of the fall of creation, human beings have struggled with ownership. When God asked Adam and Eve if they had eaten from the tree that He had commanded them not to, Adam replied, "The woman you put here with me, she gave me some fruit from the tree, and I ate it." (Genesis 3:12). Eve responded with, "The serpent deceived me, and I ate it." (Genesis 3:13). Immediately when questioned by God, both individuals deflected the blame to someone else and failed to take ownership for their decision. Unfortunately, shifting blame is a common human response to many situations for kids and adults.

In 1 Samuel 13, Saul failed to keep the commands of the Lord in battle. When Samuel asked Saul what he had done, his response was a classic example of excuse-making, "You did not come at the set time." Saul consistently prioritized his status, not God's, causing him to blame others when things didn't go well. We need to leave our pride at the door, trusting God and his purpose. We must be responsible for our actions through the good and the bad. As Matthew 5:37 states, "All you simply need to say is simply "yes" or "no," anything beyond this comes from the evil one. Don't get caught up in the blame game; own it.

Journal: Leadership is filled with highs and lows. There are times during the low points when instead of taking ownership, we shift blame to others. What can you do today to demonstrate the ownership God wants you to have for your actions? How can you foster an "extreme ownership" mentality for yourself and those you lead?

Additional Reading: 1 Samuel 13, Matthew 5:37

Day 21

•

Comparison is the Thief of Joy

Today's Verse: 1 Samuel 18:9 - And from that time on Saul kept a jealous eye on David.

One of my favorite quotes is from Teddy Roosevelt, "Comparison is the thief of joy" (Roosevelt, n.d.). Unfortunately, I have battled comparing myself to others far too often in my life. It can be easy to get distracted by the success of others, instead of focusing on the mission God has set out for us. Technology and social media make this even more challenging as we have instant access into the lives of others. As we scroll our devices or see someone else experiencing success, it can be easy to think, "Wow, he/she has accomplished that already, I wish I did that," or "I need to do more, I'm not doing enough." We begin to lose sight of our mission and focus on somebody else's.

We can also become distracted by the success of those on our own "team." After a victory over the Philistines, the Israelites were celebrated and sang, "Saul has slain his thousands, and David his ten thousands"

(v. 7). Instead of celebrating the success of Israel and his subordinate, David, Saul steamed with anger. Unlike David, Saul sought affirmation from man, not God. Saul's heart was not in a right or close relationship with the Lord. He then spent life in a jealous rage focused on David instead of serving the Almighty God and the people of Israel. As Zach Williams sings in his song, Old Church Choir, *"I've got a heart overflowing 'cause I've been restored, there ain't nothing gonna steal my joy, no, there ain't nothing gonna steal my joy"* (Williams, 2016). Don't let comparing yourself to others steal your joy.

Journal: How has comparing yourself to others negatively impacted your leadership? How can remaining focused on the mission God set out for you impact your leadership?

Additional Reading: 1 Samuel 18

Day 22

---•---

Remain Steadfast

Today's Verse: 1 Samuel 18:7 - As they danced, they sang: "Saul has slain his thousands, and David his tens of thousands."

We often experience both praise and criticism in our leadership roles. A tremendous part of leadership is the vulnerability of putting ourselves out there to be the face behind decisions. In his book, *The Power of Positive Leadership*, Jon Gordon says, "If they praise you, show up and do the work. If they criticize you, show up and do the work. If no one even notices you, just show up and do the work" (Gordon, 2017). While it is essential to listen to others, personally, I have spent too much time dwelling on the opinions of others, specifically negative opinions. It can be easy to allow success or criticism to dominate our thinking and prevent us from doing the work we've been called to do.

David was not deterred from serving the Lord whether responding to human praise and popularity or scorn and criticism. After defeating the Philistines, women danced and sang throughout the cities of Israel, celebrating David. His popularity continued to grow among the people. David must have been happy to hear those affirming words, but he did not allow them to dominate his thinking or change his ways. David was also misunderstood and publicly rebuked by his own brother, Eliab, to whom he responded gently. David's heart was in the right place to handle praise and criticism from his time out in the shepherd's field. Like David, we should seek to put the opinions of others in the proper perspective as we carry out our mission for the Lord. Never allow yourself to get too high or too low in your leadership roles, remain steadfast.

Journal: What was the last bit of praise you received as a leader? Contrary, what was the last piece of criticism you received as a leader? How did each of these opinions affect you? How can you ensure other people's opinions do not deter you from carrying out your mission for the Lord?

Additional Reading: 1 Samuel 18, 1 Samuel 17

Day 23

---•---

Someone Needs
You Today

Today's Verse: 2 Samuel 19:7 - "Now go out and encourage your men. I swear by the Lord that if you don't go out, not a man will be left with you by nightfall. This will be worse for you than all the calamities that have come upon you from your youth until now."

When I was leading as a school principal during the Covid-19 pandemic, I noticed moments when I would begin to feel sorry for myself. Whether it involved contact tracing, phone calls, upset families, ever-changing protocols, paperwork, "gray" areas, or the day-to-day stresses, I would think to myself, "What in the world am I doing?" I had moments some days when I wanted to hide. Those moments caused me to think only about myself, and I would briefly lose sight of the greater good. I have those days as a husband and a father as well! It can be easy to take our eyes off the greater good when facing various challenges. Ironically, I have found that the days I wake up and would rather hide than arise, are the days someone needs me the most.

In today's verse, King David's army had recently won a victory but David's son, Absalom, was killed. Despite the victory, David wept and mourned the death of his son. King David's grief demoralized his army because the troops who had heard it said, "The king is grieving for his son." David could have continued to sulk and mourn, but he reframed his thinking and made a decision for the greater good. "David got up and took his seat in the gateway" (v. 8). David did not feel like taking that seat and leading the army, but he knew it was the right thing to do. David put his feelings aside and went out and encouraged his army and we must do the same. Someone needs you today.

Journal: As leaders we have all had days when we felt like "hiding" due to our current emotional state or feelings of being overwhelmed. Despite those days when you feel like "hiding," how can you continue to keep your eyes on the greater good in your leadership and focus on meeting the needs of the people you lead?

Additional Reading: 2 Samuel 19

Day 24

Refuge and Strength

Today's Verse: Nehemiah 1:4 - When I heard these things, I sat down and wept. For some days I mourned and fasted and prayed before the God of heaven.

Leadership can be a roller coaster with great news one second, and difficult news the next. When we receive bad news or face challenges, where or to what do we turn? Do we turn to the cupboard for a snack? Or do we turn to entertainment, watching a movie, or binge-watching a show? How about scrolling social media to numb and delay our response to the difficulty? It can be easy to sulk and feel bad for ourselves, call someone, and complain. We all respond to bad news in different ways. While there are plenty of healthy activities we can engage in as a response to stressful situations, we should first follow Nehemiah's example after receiving tragic news.

After Nehemiah learned the survivors in Jerusalem were in great distress, and the wall of Jerusalem was broken down, he knew there was only one place he could go for refuge; he went directly to God. Nehemiah immediately began to pray and earnestly seek God in the situation. Nehemiah prayed a prayer of praise and humility, recognizing the disobedience of the Israelites and asking for God to be attentive and grant him favor and success (v. 5-11). Nehemiah waited on the Lord as he renewed his strength through prayer. After the wall was completed in fifty-two days, all the surrounding nations lost their confidence as they realized the work had been done with the help of the Lord (Nehemiah 6: 15-16). When difficulties arise, turn to the Heavenly Father for wisdom and discernment, He is your refuge and strength (Psalm 46:1).

Journal: Leaders need to be careful not to ride the emotional roller coaster of emotions. What are actions you can take in your leadership practice to cope or respond to difficult news or situations in a productive way? How can you ensure you seek the Lord first to guide you as a leader and stay off the roller coaster?

Additional Reading: Nehemiah 1, Nehemiah 6, Psalm 46:1

Day 25

Pride Goes Before Destruction

Today's Verse: 2 Chronicles 26:16 - But after Uzziah became powerful, his pride led to his downfall. He was unfaithful to the Lord his God and entered the temple of the Lord to burn incense on the altar of incense.

As I was applying and interviewing for a new job recently, I was on my knees in prayer daily. I was in the Word of God, desperate for Him, trusting Him, turning over my worries and fears to Him. I meditated on Proverbs 3:5-6: "Trust in the Lord with all your heart, lean not on your own understanding, in all your ways acknowledge him and he will direct your paths." I knew I could do nothing apart from God. The Lord blessed me with a new position and things were going well. I was experiencing moments of success, learning through the challenges, and my confidence grew. However, I became busier at work and home with more responsibilities and began spending less time praying and reading the Bible. God graciously convicted my heart, and I knew I needed to take a step back, reframe my thinking, and remember that true confidence in the Lord requires humility.

Uzziah had done what was right in the eyes of the Lord. The King feared God, and as long as he sought the Lord, God gave him success (v. 4 and 5). Uzziah had a well-trained army, defeated many nations, and his fame grew. Unfortunately, so did his pride. As today's verse states, after Uzziah became powerful, his pride led to his downfall. Ligon Duncan said, "Success inflates the ego of the natural man, but it humbles the man of God" (Duncan, 1999). Uzziah took his eyes off the Heavenly throne and began to think he could lead independently. How quickly we can go from utter dependence on God to thinking we can do it on our own. Allow success to humble you, because success is not your own. As Proverbs 16:18 states, "Pride goes before destruction."

Journal: Accomplishments often lead to pride and can unfortunately take our focus away from God. As leaders, how can you ensure you are humbly relying on God in your leadership and not pridefully trusting in yourself?

Additional Reading: 2 Chronicles 26, Proverbs 16:18, Proverbs 3:5-6

Day 26

---•---

Quick to Listen

Today's Verse: 2 Chronicles 26:18 - They confronted him and said, "It is not right for you, Uzziah, to burn incense to the Lord. That is for the priests, the descendants of Aaron, who have been consecrated to burn incense. Leave the sanctuary, for you have been unfaithful, and you will not be honored by God."

My wife and I typically prioritize spending time in conversation on Saturday mornings before the kids wake up. One morning we were discussing our family, upcoming schedules, and the current pace of life. The conversation was going well but began to take a gradual turn. At one point, my wife stopped and said, "You're not listening right now; your prideful ears are listening." Unfortunately, she was right. I took something she said personally and became defensive. The moment I became defensive, I quit listening. Why? Although what she said was the truth, it was not what I wanted to hear, and my prideful heart took over from there.

God allowed King Uzziah an opportunity to stop burning incense and leave the sanctuary. Eight courageous priests did the right thing by confronting Uzziah for his unfaithfulness and disobedience to God.

Unfortunately, it was not what Uzziah wanted to hear. Instead of listening to the wise counsel, his heart became hardened, and he became angry and raged at the priests in his presence. Much like Uzziah, when our hearts are not aligned with our Heavenly Father, we can become prideful, trust in ourselves, and lose sight of our Godly mission, significantly limiting our leadership potential. A bold prayer we can pray is found in Psalm 139 verses 23 and 24: "Search me, O God, and know my heart; test me and know my anxious thoughts. See if there is any offensive way in me, and lead me in the way everlasting." Listening is underrated; be quick to listen with a humble heart today.

Journal: Spend quiet time in honest reflection with the Lord on Psalm 139: 23-24: "Search me, O God, and know my heart; test me and know my anxious thoughts. See if there is any offensive way in me, and lead me in the way everlasting." How can a heart aligned with God transform the way you listen to others?

Additional Reading: 2 Chronicles 26, James 1:19

Day 27

———— • ————

Rooted in Your "Why"

Today's Verse: Esther 4:16 - "Go, gather together all the Jews who are in Susa, and fast for me. Do not eat or drink for three days, night or day. I and my attendants will fast as you do. When this is done, I will go to the king, even though it is against the law. And if I perish, I perish."

Here is an important comment about our purpose from the comedian Michael Jr.: *"When you know your why, your what has more impact, because you are walking in or towards your purpose"* (Wright Jr., 2017). In the YouTube video, Michael Jr. learned an audience member was a music instructor. To have some fun, he asked the audience member to sing the first part of Amazing Grace. The gentleman sang it beautifully, and the audience loved it. Michael Jr. added a little context to the "why" behind singing Amazing Grace and challenged the audience member to sing it again. Wow. The audience member took Amazing Grace to a whole other level, and the audience was on their feet in joy and celebration. His what (singing the song) had significantly more impact when he knew the "why" behind his singing.

Esther is the perfect example of knowing her "why." Esther knew she was risking her life by approaching the king, but she also went with humble confidence, knowing exactly what she needed to say and why she needed to say it. Going to the king without being called was extremely dangerous-—possibly to the point of death. However, Esther was determined to be obedient to God, no matter the cost. Esther knew her "why," and because of that, she exhibited courage, boldness, and bravery to do the right thing. "And If I perish, I perish (v. 16)," Esther knew her "why" and so should we. Remain rooted in your "why" and what you do will have significantly more impact as you walk towards your purpose.

Journal: Identify your "why" statement and write it down. Think deeply about your "why" statement. How is the Lord immersed into this statement? If the Lord is not immersed in your "why" statement, how can it be altered?

Additional Reading: Esther Chapter 4 and 5

YouTube: Know Your Why - Michael Jr.

Day 28

Turn Upward

Today's Verse: Haggai 2:23 - "On that day", declares the Lord Almighty, "I will take you, my servant Zerubbabel son of Shealtiel," declares the Lord, "and I will make you like my signet ring, for I have chosen you," declares the Lord Almighty."

One day I reached out to my wife while struggling at work after hitting a point of exhaustion accompanied by an overwhelming feeling of disillusionment. I texted my wife, "I don't know if I can do it all." It was a moment when I felt all my responsibilities as a husband, father, principal, and coach hit me at once. She wisely responded with, "The Lord did not call you to be a principal because you are equipped, but He will equip you for the job." Wow. What a humble reminder to lean into the one who has chosen me for my leadership positions. In their book, *The Gift of Disillusionment*, authors Peter Greer and Christ Horst shared that times of disillusionment are "an invitation to turn not inward but upward" (Greer & Horst, 2022). I was looking inward, and my wife reminded me to look upward.

I cannot imagine how Zerubbabel must have felt when he heard the Lord Almighty say, "I have chosen you." Zerubbabel was a faithful servant to the Lord by governing his people well and loyal in overseeing the rebuilding of the temple in Jerusalem. As we battle to overcome and endure the challenges of leadership, that same confidence can be ours because the Lord has chosen us. As Psalm 121:1-2 says: "I lift my eyes to the hills - where does my help come from? My help comes from the Lord, the Maker of heaven and earth." The next time you experience any doubt in your leadership, lift your eyes upward to the Almighty One, for he has chosen you.

Journal: As leaders, we often experience times and periods of disillusionment. Spend some time in silence pondering the Heavenly Father saying to you, "I have chosen you." How can turning upward strengthen you to face each day?

Additional Reading: Haggai 2, Psalm 121:1

Day 29

Listen First, Ask Questions, Speak Last

Today's Verse: Luke 2:46- After three days they found him (Jesus) in the temple courts, sitting among the teachers, listening to them and asking questions.

I love sitting in Sunday School class, attending conferences, and just being in the presence of those having more life experiences and wisdom than me. Whether it be their walk with the Lord, leadership experiences, parenting, or marriage, I try to be a sponge and absorb as much as possible by listening and asking questions. In those situations, I think of Jesus as a young boy sitting in the temple courts observing, listening, and learning from the wise teachers in the temple. It can become easy for leaders to think we have to be the ones talking with all the right answers. However, we should instead prioritize listening, learning, and asking the right questions.

There is not much written in the Bible about Jesus as a boy. However, this section of Luke 2 explains how Jesus grew in wisdom, stature, and favor with God and men (Luke 2:52). As a boy, Jesus surrounded himself with wise teachers in the temple courts. Luke does not say Jesus was talking at the temple courts but states that Jesus was listening and asking questions. James mentions in verse 1:19, "Everyone should be quick to listen and slow to speak." Later in the New Testament, we see how often Jesus led and transformed the hearts of others through listening and asking questions. We should never stop listening, asking questions, and learning from others as we lead. Listen first, ask questions, speak last.

Journal: As leaders we need to be able take the role of both teacher and learner as Jesus did as a child in the temple. Who can you surround yourself with to listen and learn from in order to grow in leadership wisdom? Who is seeking you out to learn from your experiences and wisdom?

Additional Reading: Luke 2, James 1:19

Day 30

Three, Twelve, Seventy-Two

Today's Verse: Matthew 4:19 - "Come follow me", Jesus said, "and I will make you fishers of men."

I am a people person and genuinely curious about people and their life stories. As I have grown in my leadership, I have met and connected with more and more people. As much as I cherish all the relationships, I learned it can be challenging to devote the same amount of time and energy to them. I tried to give everyone the same amount of time and energy early in my leadership and quickly realized it was not sustainable and limited not only my potential, but also the potential of others. I needed to recalibrate my thinking and strategically identify and grow a group of leaders around me. Leaders are in the business of developing leaders, not followers.

During Jesus' time on earth, the crowds and people demanding his attention grew daily. Jesus certainly loved them all, but they did not receive the same amount of direct interaction with him. Jesus provided a living testimony that we cannot invest the same amount of time and energy into everyone. We must identify the right people to spend the most time investing in. Jesus knew the importance of developing other leaders and called twelve men to drop everything they were doing and follow him. He knew these men would be the next generation of leaders making disciples of all nations (Matt. 28:19). Jesus also had a closer relationship with three of the disciples, Peter, James, and John, who walked with him during his most intimate times. Later, Jesus sent out a group of seventy-two people two by two ahead of him to every town he visited (Luke 10). Jesus set the perfect example, devoting intentional time in growing leaders and greatly expanding his ministry in the process. Remember: three, twelve, seventy-two as you lead.

Journal: Are you stretching yourself too thin in your leadership by trying to mentor, develop, and grow all people? Or are you not investing in growing and developing other leaders? Who can you strategically invest in and grow in their leadership and in turn, multiply growth?

Additional Reading: Luke 10, Matthew 26:36-38, Matthew 28:19

Day 31

Confront Problems, Not People

Today's Verse: Matthew 5:9 - Blessed are the peacemakers, for they will be called children of God.

A quote I focus on each day is: "Confront problems, not people." Conflict can be an antidote to growth and progress within a family, team, or organization. Personally, my natural instinct is to avoid conflict because it can be flat-out uncomfortable. Others prefer to take on conflict head-on. But guess what? When we peace "fake," the conflict usually rears its ugly head again, and when we peace "break," we destroy relationships. In his book, *The Peacemaker*, Ken Sande shares three responses when it comes to conflict: peacefaking, peacebreaking, and peacemaking (Sande, 2007). Too often, we either choose the route of running away from conflict or fighting back when conflict arises instead of using our leadership to help bring resolution to the conflict.

Satan is the enemy of peace and seeks to disrupt and stir up conflict among people. However, God desires reconciliation, and Jesus is the ultimate example of what it means to be a peacemaker. Paul reminds us in 2 Corinthians 5:18 that God has entrusted us to the ministry of reconciliation. Ultimately, with his blood on the cross, Jesus spent his time on earth seeking restoration between all of us sinners and the loving Creator, God. We ought to use Christ's example and Paul's reminder to prioritize conflict resolution in our leadership roles, whether in households, teams, or organizations. Remember, confront the problem, not the person.

Journal: Is your natural leadership tendency to peace fake, peace break, or peace make? How is your conflict response helping you? How is your conflict response holding you back? How can you ensure your conflict response positively impacts the growth of your family, team, or organization?

Additional Reading: Matthew 5, 2 Corinthians 5:18

Day 32

Reach Their Heart

Today's Verse: Matthew 22:1 - Jesus spoke to them again in parables, saying: "The kingdom of heaven is like a king who prepared a wedding banquet for his son."

When I was in my third year as an assistant principal, I remember being in the auditorium preparing to send a group of about five hundred students and staff out for our school's second annual "Going Beyond" Day of Service. It was an extraordinary event where the students gave back through service to the local school community and beyond. I kicked off the event by reviewing rules and procedures and sent the students and teachers out into the community for the day. Later, my building principal pulled me aside and asked if I would like some advice. He said, "Next time you prepare to communicate with an audience, I want you to think of a story you could tell to capture the audience's attention. What do you want them to know? How do you want them to feel? What do you want them to do?" From that time on, I have focused on what I want the audience to know, feel, and do each time I speak.

The brief interaction with my building principal transformed how I communicate with others. Jesus knew exactly how to communicate to reach the hearts of his audience. Jesus spoke through parables and stories throughout the gospels, and he was not simply going over rules and procedures and telling people exactly what to do. Still, his storytelling allowed him to reach the hearts of others to think and reflect individually. Crowds often watched and listened to Jesus in utter amazement. Let Jesus' parables and stories enable you to connect and reach the hearts of your audience as you communicate and lead.

Journal: How can Jesus' example of communicating through parables and stories impact the way you communicate with those you lead? As you approach your next conversation, meeting, or presentation, how can you incorporate the power of storytelling to help captivate your audience?

Additional Reading: Matthew 22

Day 33

Fear is a Liar

Today's Verse: Matthew 25:25 - So I was afraid and went out and hid your talent in the ground.

I have always loved the children's song, "This Little Light of Mine." Two lines that stand out to me above the rest: 1) "This little light of mine, I'm going to let it shine," and 2) "Hide it under a bush oh no, I'm going to let it shine." God often uses those innocent children's songs to connect with my heart. As I continue to grow older and face new opportunities, fear tries to creep in and prevent me from letting my God-given light shine. Satan wants to plant that seed of doubt in our minds to hide our gifts "under a bush."

In the Parable of the Talents, Jesus told the story of a man going on a journey and entrusting his property to three servants. He gave each of them according to his ability. Two servants took what they were given, let their light shine, worked hard, and gained more. The third servant returned precisely what his master had given him and said, "So I was afraid and went out and hid your talent in the ground" (v. 25). The third servant allowed fear to significantly limit what God could do in and through him and literally hid his talents underground. We must be faithful with what God gives us, the "big" and the "small," and let our lights shine and trust that He will provide. Let your God-given leadership light shine! Fear is a liar.

Journal: Fear in leadership can hold you back from sharing the talents and gifts that God has given you. How can the Parable of the Talents encourage you to choose faith over fear and respond like the first two servants?

Additional Reading: Matthew 25: 14-30, Lamentations 3:57

Day 34

Alone with God

Today's Verse: Luke 5: 15-16 - Yet the news about him spread all the more, so that crowds of people came to hear him and to be healed of their sicknesses. But Jesus often withdrew to lonely places and prayed.

I have heard my pastor, Reverend Michael Brown, share many times, "If the situation seems beyond what you can do, then you are in a perfect place for what God can do." I often find myself in that place. Whether that includes a combination of being a husband, father, coach, school leader, or in a role at church, I have felt the stress of those increased demands and responsibilities. However, when I become busier, and my responsibilities increase, I tend to spend less time alone with the Lord instead of prioritizing time with the Heavenly Father for rest, quietness, and strength,

As word of Jesus spread among the people, so did the size of the crowds that followed him, and Jesus' popularity increased dramatically during his time on earth. However, the large crowds and increased demands propelled Jesus to solitary time in prayer with his Heavenly Father, not away from it. Jesus consistently prioritized withdrawing from the large crowds and spending quiet time praying. Isaiah 30:15 says, "In repentance and rest is your salvation, in quietness and trust is your strength." Jesus knew God was his strength and needed to prioritize solitary time with Him for wisdom, refreshment, and strength. When the situation seemed beyond his control, Jesus knew exactly where to run. Take time to be alone with God; there's no better place.

Journal: Leadership demands often cause us to be consumed with the here and now and provide little time to separate from the "crowd." How do you respond to increased publicity, responsibility, and demands? How can you ensure you are withdrawing from "crowds" to the Heavenly Father?

Additional Reading: Luke 5, Isaiah 30:15

Day 35

Be Where Jesus' Feet Are

Today's Verse: Luke 10: 39-40 - She had a sister called Mary, who sat at the Lord's feet listening to what he said. But Martha was distracted by all the preparations that had to be made. She came to him and asked, "Lord, don't you care that my sister has left me to do the work by myself? Tell her to help me!"

One of my favorite phrases is, "Be where your feet are." I have a sign in my room that reads, "Be here now." However, being fully present is one of the biggest obstacles for me and many other leaders. While I seek to serve the Lord in my many roles, I take on too much and struggle to be present. While I am at work, my mind will be pulled to home, and it is easy for my mind to drift to something at work when at home. When I am at church, my mind can be pulled to everything else that needs to be done. When I fall into this cycle, I become stressed and irritable, even comparing myself to others as I attempt to serve the Lord. In those moments, I miss being fully present with the people right in front of me and fail to rest at the feet of Jesus.

As Jesus and his disciples were traveling, a woman named Martha opened her home to them. As Mary was fully present, sitting at the feet of Jesus, Martha was distracted with serving and preparations. Martha did nothing wrong in working hard for Jesus. Still, she became irritable when she focused on what Mary was not doing and was distracted from Jesus. Charles Spurgeon states, "Martha's frustration is typical of those who diligently serve with good intent but forget to also sit at Jesus' feet" (Spurgeon, n.d.). Presence is a superpower that many of us do not have, and it begins by following Mary's example of "being where Jesus' feet are."

Journal: Leadership can be an "all consuming" endeavor. How has serving (even for the Lord) caused you to become distracted and irritable, instead of sitting at the feet of Jesus? How can today's passage alter your approach?

Additional Reading: Luke 10:41

Day 36

———— • ————

Prioritize People

Today's Verse: John 10:14 - I am the good shepherd: I know my sheep and my sheep know me.

A leadership mantra of mine is, "It's all about people." However, far too often, I let my to-do list get in the way of putting people first. One Friday evening, my wife shared that she did not want to see my laptop out that upcoming weekend. Unfortunately, she found me on my computer trying to sneak in work the next day. I could tell she wasn't happy, and I shared there was just "one more thing I needed to finish." She said, "Zac, you always say there is one more thing you need to finish. Look around; what do you see?" To set the stage, my wife was a stay-at-home mom with our three young kids, ages nine, six, and four. As I peered around the room, I saw a pile of laundry, clothes requiring ironing, toys on the floor, and various other tasks still needing to be finished. She said, "Do you know what would suffer if I always focused on just needing to finish one more thing?" I humbly paused and listened. "The relationships with the kids and our relationship would suffer. There's always going to be something that still needs to be done, whether at work or home, but we need to focus on the people around us."

As the "good shepherd," Jesus set the ultimate example of prioritizing people. In today's verse, Jesus describes himself as the "good shepherd," and the sheep are the people. Jesus knew the importance of relationships and taking the time to get to others. When thinking of a herd of sheep, it's easy to think of the sheep as all the same. A good shepherd knows that all the sheep are different with their unique personalities and characteristics. The shepherd must prioritize getting to know each sheep and what each one needs. The sheep are then able to understand and trust their shepherd. The same is true in our leadership roles; prioritize getting to know people and the people getting to know you; the to-do list will always be there.

Journal: It can be easy for leaders to get caught up in our to-do lists and task completion, causing us to miss what's most important: people. How can Jesus' example of the "good shepherd" help you prioritize getting to know the people you lead? How can truly knowing people impact the way you lead daily?

Additional Reading: John 10

Day 37

---•---

Thinking of Yourself Less

Today's Verse: John 13:5 - After that, he (Jesus) poured water into a basin and began to wash his disciples' feet, drying them with the towel that was wrapped around his waist.

My family gathers for dinner at my parents' house on Sunday evenings. It is a time to gather, relax, eat, and fellowship with one another. At one meal, something caught my eye; my brother-in-law waited until everyone was served their meal before he got his. I started to keep an eye out for this each week, and as expected, he waited until everyone was served before he fixed his plate. Can you guess where we could find him after dinner? At the sink, gathering and washing dishes as family members finished their meals. My brother-in-law certainly has a heart of service in all that he does. Authentic servant leaders operate from a position of humility and seek to put others before themselves. Unfortunately for me, servant leadership is easier said than done.

Jesus is the ultimate example of a servant leader. The time was near for him to be beaten, tortured, and left to die on a wooden cross.

However, in those moments leading up to his crucifixion, Jesus did not think of himself; he thought of his twelve disciples. That evening he did something the disciples thought was crazy; he got up from the table, got on his knees, and washed their feet. At a time when most, if not all of us, would be thinking of ourselves, Jesus began to do the job of the lowest servant in the household. As Matthew 20:28 says, "Just as the Son of Man did not come to be served, but to serve, and to give his life as a ransom for many." Jesus did not just speak about true humility; he showed it. As C.S. Lewis said, "Humility is not thinking less of yourself, it's thinking of yourself less" (Lewis, n.d.).

Journal: Leaders are blessed with having many opportunities to serve others. What opportunities, large or small, do you anticipate coming to you today to show Christ's love by serving others?

Additional Reading: John 13, Matthew 20:28

Day 38

---•---

Who's Coming with You?

Today's Verse: Mark 14:32-34 - They went to a place called Gethsemane, and Jesus said to his disciples, "Sit here while I pray." He took Peter, James, and John along with him, and he began to be deeply distressed and troubled. "My soul is overwhelmed with sorrow to the point of death," he said to them. "Stay here and keep watch."

In 2015 I unexpectedly began to battle significant anxiety and depression. I had no idea what was happening, but I would awake in the middle of the night, heart pounding, sweating, and unable to fall back asleep. My mind would race with worries and fears throughout the day and night. I thought I needed to have it all together for my family, work, and friends, so I tried to battle the feelings all by myself, and the anxiousness and depression worsened. In leadership, we often think we need to remain strong, not show "weakness," or ask for help. However, the best thing we can do is open up and bring trusted family and friends along with us during difficult times. As I began to turn to God and open up to a few family members and close friends, I began to feel the restoration process taking place and the impact of those relationships.

When Jesus was feeling "sorrow to the point of death," he took others with him. Jesus knew the importance of not only talking to his Heavenly Father, but he knew the significance of being in community and bringing others along with him during his journey here on earth. When Jesus was about to face crucifixion on the cross, he brought three trusted disciples along with him while he prayed during his time of deep sorrow. Solomon says in Ecclesiastes 3:12, "Though one may be overpowered, two can defend themselves. A cord of three strands is not quickly broken." Jesus exemplified the idea that we were not meant to go through painful situations alone. So who's coming with you?

Journal: Leadership can be a lonely position if you allow it. Do you try to navigate difficult situations alone? Identify some trusted family and friends that you can make part of your "inner circle" as you run the race God has marked out for you.

Is there something going on in your life that would alleviate a significant amount of internal anxiety if you opened up to someone?

Additional reading: Mark 14, Ecclesiastes 3:12

Day 39

---•---

Audience of One

Today's Verse: Mark 15: 3-5 - The chief priests accused him of many things. So again Pilate asked him, "Aren't you going to answer? See how many things they are accusing you of." But Jesus made no reply, and Pilate was amazed.

One of the worst feelings is to be accused of something completely false. It can be easy to take things personally, get defensive, defend ourselves, and respond to the critics. If there were one hundred things said about me regarding an action or decision, and ninety-nine are positive, while only one is critical, harmful, and inaccurate, guess which one sticks with me the most? You guessed it—the one critical comment. My natural human instinct is to explain and defend myself so that all one hundred would see and support why an action was taken, or a decision was made. We often waste a significant amount of time and brain space attempting to control things outside of our mission and control.

While many followed Jesus in amazement, listening to his teachings, searching for healing, witnessing miracles, and being in his presence, Jesus also had many critics. Even moments before crucifixion on the cross, Jesus exemplified his wisdom by not responding to his critics. Pilate allowed Jesus the opportunity to respond to his critics, and he made no reply. Pilate watched in amazement as he knew that the accusations against Jesus were false and he had done absolutely nothing to deserve death on the cross. In his devotion *Morning and Evening*, Charles Spurgeon said, "Is not patient silence the best reply to a contentious world?" (Spurgeon, n.d.). Jesus knew his mission here on earth, and he rested in his audience of one, his Heavenly Father. Go and do the same.

Journal: As leaders, we can at times become victims of others' lies or rumors about us. How can Jesus' response in Mark 15:5, "*But Jesus still made no reply,*" give you confidence in your leadership when others' speaking inaccurate or falsely about you?

Additional Reading: Mark 15

Day 40

———— • ————

Encourage, Encourage, Encourage

Today's Verse: 1 Thessalonians 5:11 - Therefore encourage one another and build each other up, just as in fact you are doing.

The late founder of Chick-fil-A, S. Truett Cathy, was fond of saying, "How do you know if someone needs encouragement? If they are breathing" (Cathy, n.d.). Today's verse from Thessalonians is one of my life verses that I refer to daily. The definition of encouragement is *the action of giving someone support, confidence, or hope*. Everyone has a "story," and it is essential to genuinely get to know others, learn their stories, and walk alongside them with encouragement in leadership. Leadership is about growing people, whether employees, players, coaches, or family members, but before *growing* people, we must focus on *knowing* people to encourage them in their journey.

In today's verse, Paul is speaking to the Thessalonians about the coming of the Lord. In this passage, Paul spoke multiple times about the importance of encouraging one another to remain alert and self-controlled. Additionally, encourage each other to not grieve like the rest of the men who had no hope (v.13). Most importantly, Paul reminded the Thessalonians to encourage one another and remain focused on the mission set out before them. It is easy to get distracted and lose sight along the way, and leaders must create a culture of encouragement. We can all use support, confidence, and hope; we all need a little encouragement. Now go out with confidence, encouraging one another as we all "run the race" God has marked out for us! (Hebrews 12:1)

Journal: Encouragement is the fuel to keep people thriving and remaining hopeful. How can today's verse on encouragement transform your leadership and the culture of your family, school, team, or organization as you lead? What is something you can do today to encourage those you lead?

Additional Reading: 1 Thessalonians 5, Hebrews 12:1

Afterword

The 40-day journey together is complete, but our leadership journey is far from over. My hope is that the last 40 days have helped prepare you to stare the challenges of leadership in the face through humility and confidence rooted only in God's word and prayer.

I want to conclude this devotional book by sharing lyrics to a song that has been instrumental in my leadership, specifically as I spent time writing this book. The song is "Confidence" by Sanctus Real (Sanctus Real, 2018). I would encourage you to spend time listening to the song and reflecting on the words as you prepare to go out and lead with humble confidence!

I'm not a warrior
I'm too afraid to lose
I feel unqualified for what you're callin' me to
But Lord with your strength
I've got no excuse
'Cause broken people are exactly who you use

So, give me faith like Daniel in the lion's den
Give me hope like Moses in the wilderness
Give me a heart like David, Lord be my defense
So, I can face my giants with confidence

You took a shepherd boy
And made him a King
So, I'm gonna trust you and give you everything
I'll be a conqueror
'Cause you fight for me
I'll be a champion claiming your victory

Give me faith like Daniel in the lion's den
Give me hope like Moses in the wilderness
Give me a heart like David, Lord be my defense
So, I can face my giants with confidence

I'm gonna sing and shout and shake the walls
I won't stop until I see 'em fall
Gonna stand up, step out when you call
Jesus, Jesus
I'm gonna sing and shout and shake the walls
I won't stop until I see 'em fall
Gonna stand up, step out when you call
Jesus

Give me faith like Daniel in the lion's den
Give me hope like Moses in the wilderness
Give me a heart like David, Lord be my defense
So, I can face my giants with confidence (Yeah)
Give me faith like Daniel in the lion's den
Give me hope like Moses in the wilderness
Give me a heart like David, Lord be my defense
So, I can face my giants with confidence
I'll face my giants with confidence

References

Armstrong, M., Hulse, E., Lolli, D., Rohman, C. (2018). Confidence [Recorded by Sanctus Real]. On *Changed*. Framework, Provident Distribution.

C. H. Spurgeon: Spurgeon's sermons volume 52: 1906 - Christian Classics Ethereal Library. (n.d.). Retrieved June 18, 2022, from https://ccel.org/ccel/spurgeon/sermons52/sermons52.xl.html

Duncan, L. (1999, June 6) *The establishment of a covenant people: The covenant continues (the life of isaac) (1) the search for a bride*. LigonDuncan.com. Retrieved June 18, 2022, from https://ligonduncan.com/the-establishment-of-a-covenant-people-the-covenant-continues-the-life-of-isaac-1-the-search-for-a-bride-971/

Dungy, T., & Whitaker, N. (2011). *The one year uncommon life daily challenge*. Tyndale Momentum.

Fadling, A. (2017). *An unhurried leader: The Lasting Fruit of daily influence*. IVP Books, an imprint of InterVarsity Press.

Fullan, M. (2011). *Change leader: Learning to do what matters most*. Jossey-Bass.

Gordon, J. (2017). *The power of positive leadership*. John Wiley & Sons Inc.

Hulse, E., Wedgeworth, C., Williams, Z. (2016). Old Church Choir [Recorded by Williams, Z.]. On *Chain Breaker*. Essential.

Goodreads. (n.d.). *A quote by C.S. Lewis.* Goodreads. Retrieved June 18, 2022, from https://www.goodreads.com/quotes/7288468-humility-is-not-thinking-less-of-yourself-it-s-thinking-of

Greer, P., & Horst, C. (2022). *The gift of disillusionment: Enduring hope for leaders after idealism fades.* Bethany House Publishers, a division of Baker Publishing Group.

Kuiper, M., McKeehan, T. (2021). Help is on the way [Recorded by McKeehan, T.]. *On Beat of My Heart.* ForeFront, Capitol CMG.

LifeChurchtv. (2018, December 10). *Letting go of distractions - travel light, part 2 with pastor Craig Groeschel.* YouTube. Retrieved June 18, 2022, from https://www.youtube.com/watch?v=51MAxagbuOA&t=30s

Lucado, M. (2021, October 1). *Nothing is too hard for him.* FaithGateway. Retrieved June 18, 2022, from https://www.faithgateway.com/nothing-is-too-hard-for-him/#.Yq3cKezMJb8

Maxwell, J. C. (2015). *The leadership handbook: 26 critical lessons every leader needs.* Nelson Books, an imprint of Thomas Nelson.

Merriam-Webster. (n.d.). *Delegate definition & meaning.* Merriam-Webster. Retrieved June 18, 2022, from https://www.merriam-webster.com/dictionary/delegate

Miller, S. (2003). *C.H. Spurgeon on spiritual leadership.* Moody Publishers.

Nieuwhof, C. (2022, February 2). *Exhaustion is the gateway drug to _____. (moral failure + 6 other unintended consequences).* CareyNieuwhof.com. Retrieved June 18, 2022, from https://careynieuwhof.com/exhaustion-gateway-drug-to-moral-failure/

Parke, B. (2019, April 2.). *Who said "comparison is the thief of joy" & how is it represented in the Bible?* biblestudytools.com. Retrieved June 18, 2022, from https://www.biblestudytools.com/bible-study/topical-studies/who-said-comparison-is-the-thief-of-joy.html

Sande, K. (2007). *The peacemaker: A biblical guide to resolving personal conflict.* Baker Books.

Segal, M. (2021, September 2). *You have time to sit with god*. Desiring God. Retrieved June 18, 2022, from https://www.desiringgod.org/articles/you-have-time-to-sit-with-god

Spurgeon, C. H. (2018). *Morning and evening: Daily readings*. Wilder Publications, LLC.

S. Truett Cathy quote. A. (n.d.). Retrieved June 18, 2022, from https://www.azquotes.com/quote/919164

Stanley, A. (2006). *The next generation leader: Five essentials for those who will shape the future*. Struik Christian Books.

THEMICHAELJRSHOW. (2017, January 8). *Know your why | Michael Jr.*. YouTube. Retrieved June 18, 2022, from https://www.youtube.com/watch?v=1ytFB8TrkTo&t=44s

Tripp, P. D. (2010). *What did you expect?: Redeeming the realities of marriage*. Crossway.

Tripp, P. D. (2013, December 29). Trading one dramatic resolution for 10,000 little ones. Desiring God. . Retrieved June 18, 2022, from https://www.desiringgod.org/articles/trading-one-dramatic-resolution-for-10000-little-ones

Zondervan. (2009). *Holy bible: New international version*.

Acknowledgments

We are not made to run our race alone; rather, we are made to be in community with one another, cheering each other on. I would like to thank and recognize the many people who have helped me on this leg of my race:

+ To Jimmy Casas, Dr. Jeffrey Zoul, and everyone at ConnectEDD Publishing. Thank you for believing in the vision of this project and making it a reality. I am grateful for all your leadership, wisdom, and guidance throughout the process.

+ To the wonderful people who read a draft of the book and offered their time, feedback, perspective, and encouragement. Thank you!
    ◊ Carly Bauermaster
    ◊ Art Paynter
    ◊ Mike Hammel
    ◊ Jessica Prokay
    ◊ Ahna Fulmer
    ◊ Jay Scott

+ To my parents, Scott and Susie, there hasn't been a day that I haven't known Jesus. Thank you!

+ To my grandmothers, Faye Wade, Nancy Bauermaster, and the late Jane Bauermaster. Thank you for your steadfast leadership in Jesus. You have led our family by example for generations to come.

+ To my brother-in-laws, Mike Hammel and Adam Blevins, "As iron sharpens iron, so one man sharpens another" (Proverbs 27:17). Thank you for sharpening me.

+ To my pastor and friend, Michael Brown. I am grateful God brought you and your family to Quarryville, Pennsylvania. God has used your preaching, teaching, and friendship as a tremendous tool for shaping my heart and leadership.

+ To the many school leaders, teachers, and coaches who have invested in me. Thank you.

+ Most importantly, I would like to thank my Lord and Savior, Jesus Christ. He is the vine, I am the branch, apart from Him I can do nothing (John 15:5).

About the Author

Zac Bauermaster is an educational leader passionate about people. Zac's mission field is public education. One of his main tag lines is, "It's all about people." His leadership style exemplifies a people-first approach as he seeks to glorify God in all he does. Zac has gained humble confidence through his daily pattern of prayer and reading scripture that he aims to share with others to advance God's kingdom.

Zac currently serves as principal at Kissel Hill Elementary School, located in the Warwick School District in Lancaster County, Pennsylvania. Zac has the tremendous opportunity to lead teachers, support staff, families, and most importantly, the next generation daily. His greatest joy in education is watching adults leverage their God-given talents and abilities through inspiring kids to find and use their gifts. Before becoming a principal, Zac served public education in various K-12 roles such as assistant principal, administrator of online learning, teacher, and coach. These experiences have grown Zac's sphere of influence and allowed him the opportunity to develop and maintain lifelong relationships.

Zac received his undergraduate degree from Millersville University in secondary education and completed his Master's Degree in Educational Technology from Pennsylvania State University. Zac returned to Penn State, where he earned his Principal Certification. Most recently, Zac earned his Doctorate in Educational Leadership and Superintendent Letter of Eligibility from Drexel University. He is a lifelong learner, always looking to learn and grow. His family jokes that he went to school in Kindergarten and hasn't ever stopped.

Zac continues to grow his leadership influence and share encouragement and positivity, along with the good news of Christ through various social media platforms, magazine publications, and speaking events.

Most importantly, Zac is a husband to his wife Carly, and father to three young kids, Olivia, Eliot, and Isaac. Zac is a firm believer in leading his family first. The family resides in Lancaster County, Pennsylvania.

More from ConnectEDD Publishing

Since 2015, ConnectEDD has worked to transform education by empowering educators to become better-equipped to teach, learn, and lead. What started as a small company designed to provide professional learning events for educators has grown to include a variety of services to help teachers and administrators address essential challenges. ConnectEDD offers instructional and leadership coaching, professional development workshops focusing on a variety of educational topics, a roster of nationally recognized educator associates who possess hands-on knowledge and experience, educational conferences custom-designed to meet the specific needs of schools, districts, and state/national organizations, and ongoing, personalized support, both virtually and onsite. In 2020, ConnectEDD expanded to include publishing services designed to provide busy educators with books and resources consisting of practical information on a wide variety of teaching, learning, and leadership topics. Please visit us online at connecteddpublishing.com or contact us at: info@connecteddpublishing.com

Recent Publications:

Live Your Excellence: Action Guide by Jimmy Casas

Culturize: Action Guide by Jimmy Casas

Daily Inspiration for Educators: Positive Thoughts for Every Day of the Year by Jimmy Casas

Eyes on Culture: Multiply Excellence in Your School by Emily Paschall

Pause. Breathe. Flourish. Living Your Best Life as an Educator by William D. Parker

L.E.A.R.N.E.R. Finding the True, Good, and Beautiful in Education by Marita Diffenbaugh

Educator Reflection Tips Volume II: Refining Our Practice by Jami Fowler-White

Handle With Care: Managing Difficult Situations in Schools with Dignity and Respect by Jimmy Casas and Joy Kelly

Disruptive Thinking: Preparing Learners for Their Future by Eric Sheninger

Permission to be Great: Increasing Engagement in Your School by Dan Butler

Daily Inspiration for Educators: Positive Thoughts for Every Day of the Year, Volume II by Jimmy Casas

The 6 Literacy Levers: Creating a Community of Readers by Brad Gustafson

The Educator's ATLAS: Your Roadmap to Engagement by Weston Kieschnick

In This Season: Words for the Heart by Todd Nesloney, LaNesha Tabb, Tanner Olson, and Alice Lee

ConnectEDD PUBLISHING

www.ingramcontent.com/pod-product-compliance
Lightning Source LLC
Chambersburg PA
CBHW070727130626
46553CB00005B/2181